T0065601

Who Is Jesus

Glenn Vellekamp

authorHOUSE®

AuthorHouse™
1663 Liberty Drive
Bloomington, IN 47403
www.authorhouse.com
Phone: 1 (800) 839-8640

Published by AuthorHouse   08/08/2016

ISBN: 978-1-5246-2350-0 (sc)
ISBN: 978-1-5246-2349-4 (e)

CONTENTS

INTRODUCTION

Why another book about the real Jesus? Isn't the Bible enough? "We have two thousand years of tradition, church history, Christmas and Easter; so why another book to tell us who you think Jesus is"? These are valid questions. The reason there have been so many books, videos, movies, TV series and seminars about Jesus, is because "orthodox" church history and tradition have left us still wondering, "What was Jesus really like"?

We can choose the Roman Catholic version or the Protestant version. We have the "oneness" Pentecostal view or the Trinitarian. We also have paintings and sculptures of what we think he looked like. We want to know. When we discuss these things, we pretty much "believe" what we believe because we believe it. Someone said, "A man hears what he wants to hear and disregards the rest". This book is for you. Since you were interested in the title and have read this much, you still have strong desire to learn more of who Jesus is. You are probably one of those who has an insatiable appetite for truth, whether it be history, just the facts or the original language. Conspiracies intrigue us because we know they expose lies, and we crave truth. I've attempted to make this book all about who Jesus says he is. However, if that was the case, all we would need would be the Bible. So I've included questions based on what we think, because we tend to add knowledge to what we already "know" and if we already "know" something and it's not fact or truth, well, we'll never find the truth. The final answer is Jesus' own words. Period.

Recently, we went to the airport to travel to Tulsa from Florida. They cancelled the flight, so we drove back home. On the way we stopped for gas and I mentioned to the young lady behind the counter that our flight was cancelled. She said, "Where were you going"? Mind you this is in July and it's near a hundred degrees outside. I said, "Tulsa" and she said, "Oh. Is it snowing"? Maybe she didn't pay attention in geography class. Or maybe she wasn't really thinking just attaching information to information. Usually when you hear "Flights are cancelled" it's because of snow, blizzards, etc. So, without thinking about it she just put the two together. I thought this was really strange, until. Until I had a conversation with a friend a week later who goes skiing in Colorado and had a bad knee injury. He said he was going to Colorado and I said, "Not skiing, I hope"? To which he said, "Not in July". I felt stupid. I don't like feeling stupid, or even misinformed. I guess I just thought the mountains had snow all the time.

The point is we have to face our misconceptions based on what Jesus says about himself, no matter how it makes us feel. Jesus is the TRUTH. I'm not saying my conclusions are the absolute truth, just that these conclusions are based on what Jesus said, not tradition, and what <u>he</u> said is absolute truth. Please read prayerfully.

1

WHO DO YOU SAY THAT I AM

In Matthew 16:13, Jesus asked his disciples who people say that he is. Some thought that he was John the Baptist or Elijah or Jeremiah or one of the prophets. It has been basically the same since. We don't hear that he is someone who has died and come back like these people mentioned but we do hear things like, "He was a prophet" or "He was a teacher" or "He was a Jewish Rabbi". But the "Christian" answer in any denomination always reiterates Peter's response when he was asked, "But you, whom do you say me to be"? Peter said, "You are the Christ, the Son of the living God". Jesus said that his Father in heaven revealed that to him, in other words, "Yes, that's right". So there we have it. That is who Jesus is, according to his own words. Yet, in "Christianity" we have different ideas about what that means and whole denominations built on the understanding or misunderstanding of who he is. So what did Peter mean when he said that? What did Jesus mean when he confirmed it? And dear reader, "Who do you say that he is"?

1

We, Christians that is, would all agree with Peter's words. But clearly that means different things to different people. For Peter and the eleven others that didn't mean that Jesus wasn't Joseph's son, according to the flesh. In John 1: 45, when Philip finds Nathanael, he says, "We have found the one whom Moses wrote about in the Law and the Prophets, Jesus the son of Joseph from Nazareth. They didn't even know that he was born in Bethlehem. Aside from Matthew 1:18-20 and Luke 1:26-35, we wouldn't know that either. Neither Matthew nor Luke was written for another 30 or 40 years after Peter was asked this question and how they knew about the angel and Mary's encounter is not known. What we do know is that no one talked about it until it was written and even after that it was years before it was dispersed. The point is that who they thought Jesus was before his resurrection, when this answer was given might be different than who they thought he was after he rose from the dead. Today we find ourselves in the same predicament; that Jesus is the Son of God means different things to different people in different denominations. So the question, "Who is Jesus"? And specifically, "Who do you say that he is"?

Jesus asked the Pharisees, "What do you think about the Christ? Whose son is he"? They said, "David's". He said to them, "Then how does David in spirit call him Lord............. if David calls him Lord, how is he his son?" No one! No one was able to answer him a word (Mt 22: 42-46). So probably the best way to know the true character of Jesus is to let him tell us. Jesus' words about himself will lead us to truth, because he is the truth. Jesus' words are spirit and they are life. Jesus' words are eternal. They will never pass away. So we can study his words and his actions and let that correct our thinking, no matter what we thought or have been taught before.

Names are important. Names were more important in Jesus' day than they are today. People actually believed that a person's name had much to do with his character. We can recall sometimes that a person's name was changed because of his character. Peter's name was changed from Simon to Cephas (pronounced Kay-fus in Aramaic), which is translated Peter in English, meaning "rock". Bartholomew was Nathanael. Joses was named Bar-Nabus by the apostles meaning son - of consolation. Levi became Matthew. James and John were "the sons of thunder". So not only were names changed to describe the character but they have also been translated into different languages and spellings. The English version of Jacob is James. Even the name "Jesus" has been translated. And more than one person was named Jesus. However, the Jesus we're talking about is the one who was named Jesus because he would "save" his people from their sins. Now there's a mouthful, because we know only God can forgive sins. The word for save in Jesus' native tongue, Hebrew, is "Yesua" (English transliteration, 3443 in the Strong's Hebrew dictionary) and it literally means to save, rescue, deliver or help. This name in Hebrew was given to Jesus because he would "save" his people. Today baby boys are named this because they honor what the "Savior" did. So in Spanish especially in Mexico there are many named, "Jesus", (pronounced Hay Sooss). In English, especially in America there are many named, "Joshua", the exact same name. They are not saviors however. So when we say "Jesus" now, we have to define what we mean. Yahweh is God's name and Yeshua or "God saves" is God's name focusing on salvation. Yeshua or Joshua or Jesus is God's name, but it has also been given to many men. Yeshua fought the battle at Jericho in the book of the Bible named after him. We know him as Joshua. In the King James Version of the Bible in Hebrews chapter 4 referring to Joshua it is translated "Jesus" in English, and "Iesous" in the original Greek (Heb 4:8). All of this to say that just because someone is named Jesus or Joshua doesn't mean he is the savior or that he is God. The baby boy that Mary birthed was named Jesus because the fullness of the Godhead dwelled in him. The baby that grew into a man was not God, but the Spirit in him is God, the fullness of God. The baby was flesh and blood, mortal, corruptible flesh. God is eternal, immortal and incorruptible. God is infinite. That means without beginning and without end. It is impossible for God to die because he is infinite. When the man, named Jesus died on the cross at Calvary, God didn't die. The man, the body God made for himself to dwell in, Jesus, gave up the Spirit and then the man died. Then God raised him up with an immortal, incorruptible,eternal body, a heavenly body, the one he had before the world was created, never to die again. We will get one of those also, when Jesus comes back or when we die physically.

So when we refer to Jesus, like the Bible does, we have to be clear as to whom we are referring. Is it the Spirit, God, "Jesus", in the man, the Messiah (Christ in Greek)? Or is it the man named Jesus. I find it easier to refer to the man as Jesus Christ or Christ Jesus or just Christ and to refer to the Spirit of God in the man as Jesus. They are inseparable, at least as long as the man was living. When Christ gave up the Spirit, he died. But God raised him up.

So who is Jesus? Are you referring to God or the man? So we assume that we know who God is, and we can see his character all through the Bible. But the divisions in "Christ-ianity" come from arguments about who the man, Jesus, is. And probably when you first saw the title of this book, you were thinking about the man that died on the cross, the man.

Some think it is disrespectful to say that the flesh of Christ is not God. They think this is denying the divinity of Christ. The divinity of Christ is that he is from above. The divinity of Christ is that he is the beginning of the creation of God. Christ is a created being in whom the eternal Son of God dwelt. The Son of God is Spirit. He is Holy. He is eternal. The man, Christ was not eternal. He had a beginning. He was created, but not from earth nor a descendant of Adam through Joseph nor Mary. The man Christ Jesus is the body God made for himself before he created anything else. When God created the heavens and the earth, it was through this body. It was an immortal body. Father created a body, that he could put the regeneration of himself in, the regeneration of himself being his Son, Spirit. But they are one and the same. The Father is the Son and they are Spirit, Holy Spirit. The Father is omnipresent, everywhere at the same time, omniscient or all knowing and omnipotent, all powerful. The Son, <u>in the body</u> called Christ is confined, not omnipresent; he learned, so not omniscient, and at times could not do many mighty works among the people, not all powerful. God limited himself as Son when he "took on" flesh, when he came in the "likeness" of sinful flesh. But make no mistake he was never sinful, nor could he be. The Son could only do what he sees the Father doing, because the Son is the Father confined to a body. The body is not the Son. The body is only a vessel, a vehicle for the Spirit to operate through. And as God designed the human body in his image, we are not our bodies either. We are spirit beings in a body. This outward shell that we live in will one day be replaced with a glorified, redeemed body. That body will not be us either, only a vessel that we will live in.

We have to get used to the idea that God is a Spirit. And most of the time we're not sure what a spirit is exactly. We might think that it's like a ghost. The original Greek word for spirit is "pneuma" from where we get pneumonia, relating to wind or breath, it is translated, "ghost" in the older versions of the Bible, such as Holy Ghost. But if all we have is images in our minds of apparitions, things we see with our physical eyes then we're off track. You can't see a spirit. "But.............."? I know, there are lots of "buts" here. Just know that you can't see a spirit. No man has seen God at any time........because God is a Spirit. So just what is a spirit then? Jesus said, "The pneuma (Greek 4151 in Strong's meaning breath or wind) pneumas (breaths or blows) where he desires and you hear his voice ; but you do not know from where he comes or where he goes-- so is everyone who is born of the pneuma. When someone speaks, breath comes out of his mouth with the voice. You can hear the voice but you can't see his breath......well unless it's really cold. Even then, you're not seeing his breath but the condensation of the moisture with his breath or a manifestation. Something in the physical that helps us see the invisible is a manifestation. The man Christ Jesus is a manifestation of God. Christ Jesus is the image of the invisible God. Angels are spirits; what people see are manifestations of angels. This is important to understand. Spirits are not physical. And if you are born of Spirit, then you are not physical either. You are a spirit in a physical body. God limited himself to a body, but not all of God was in the body. God is everywhere. The Son was in the body. There is God the Father, everywhere, and God the Son, in a body, and of course God is a Holy Spirit. Father is everywhere all the time. The Son, which is Spirit confined to a body, is in one place at a time.

The Holy Spirit is a deposit in us when we are born of Spirit until we receive new bodies. "Oh, so there are three Spirits". No. God is a Spirit. The fullness of the Spirit lives in Christ, because the body God made for himself was made in heaven, not of earth, neither descended from Adam. It was immortal and not able to sin. Adam was of the earth where Satan already existed when Adam was created out of the earth and consequently was able to sin. Evidently. When "The Angel of the Lord" (Christ) appeared to Abraham, Isaac, Jacob, Joshua, Hagar, Solomon and many others, it was in this immortal body. He appeared and disappeared. He was called Melchizedek, without father and without mother. But when God planted the DNA seed of his body in Mary it became mortal, but still not able to sin. Jesus Christ is from above not of the earth. He is called the "second man" by Paul and unlike "the first man" is not of the earth but is the Lord from heaven (1 Cor 15:45-47). Who is Jesus? The first thing we have to ask ourselves is, "Do you mean the spirit"? or, "Do you mean the man"? "Jesus" is God's name, well, the English version of the Hebrew, "YeShua", which means, "God (YHWH) saves". Christ came in his

Father's name, Jesus. So the Spirit of God, the Holy Spirit whose name is above all names, Jesus, was in the body called the Messiah or in Greek, Christ. Jesus was in Christ and so we call him Jesus Christ. Paul put it this way, "God was in Christ reconciling the world unto himself" (2 Cor 5:19. original language). This all sounds very analytical and semantic, but it is necessary if we want to know if we are referring to Spirit or man.

At this point is where all the arguments and "heresies" come in. Some say that Jesus is only a man. Some say that he is only a spirit. Every known heresy about the "divinity of Christ" enters here. And the tendency among "theologians" and dogmatic doctrinal religious analysts is to put everything that is other than what they believe into a category of some known heresy. Let the words of Jesus be the final answer. Jesus explains body, soul and spirit. If we can find agreement in the other parts of the Bible that supports what Jesus said then let's use it. But if we find any discrepancy, then let's just know that what the apostles wrote was what they knew in part. Paul said that God's ways were past finding out… (Rom 11:33), past finding out for Paul, past finding out for us, but not past finding out for Jesus, because he is God. Jesus told his apostles after he rose from the dead that a spirit does not have flesh and bone. That's man not spirit. He also said to Nicodemus, "That which is born of flesh is flesh and that which is born of spirit is spirit"(John 3).

Confusion comes in when we refer to the man, the body, as Jesus and at the same time refer to the spirit as Jesus, i.e. "Jesus died on the cross". Well, the spirit didn't die. The man died. This is difficult because in our finite minds we need to separate body from spirit to make sense of this but they are not separate until the spirit leaves the body and the body without the spirit is dead. We could think of it this way, God planted a single cell of his body's DNA that he created in heaven into Mary. Within that cell was his Spirit, the Son, the eternal spiritual Son. As the cell divided into two, the spirit was in both cells but not two spirits, and then four and then eight and so on. So the spirit is in every cell of Christ; they are inseparable, that is, until death. We could look at it this way. God is Spirit and God created matter. The first matter God created was a body for him to dwell in. This is what is meant by Jesus Christ being the beginning of the creation of God (Rev 3:14). Everything else was created through him. But the Creator is never the created. So the body God created for himself was not God, but his body, matter, flesh and bone. However, that body was not descended from Adam but was created in the beginning. Conversely, Adam was created through Jesus Christ. Whenever Jesus appeared to man, Adam, Abraham, Jacob, Solomon it was in this body, the immortal body of Jesus called Melchizedek. But when the fullness of time had come to be born of a woman the body had to be reduced, reduced to a single cell. The Spirit of God was in that single cell. The Spirit of God was in every fiber of every component of that cell. The Spirit was in the chromosomes, in the genes, in the smallest part man can discover. And when that cell was placed in Mary and attached to her uterine wall it became mortal. The immortal matter became mortal. And when it began to split into two, both cells contained the Spirit of God. The matter was not God but the Spirit became intertwined with the matter and was never separated until Jesus said, "It is finished". He became sin. The body became

9

sin. He became like Adam after Adam sinned, dead to God, and he cried out "Why have you forsaken me"? Because the Spirit of God that was in every fiber of his being was gone. The only spirit Christ had left was the spirit of man that was dead to God just like Adam. He who knew no sin became sin. And God forsook him. This is what Jesus dreaded the night before when he sweat great drops like blood. This is why he said, "Take this cup from me", (If there's any other way) but not my will...... He was dreading being separated from the Spirit. He wasn't afraid of dying. The Holy Spirit of the Son returned to Father, leaving the son of man, the flesh, the matter forsaken to bear the sin of the world. God did this willingly to pay for our redemption. His body became mortal so that it could die for our punishment which the human race deserved because of Adam's sin. But then God raised up that mortal body back to immortality by the resurrection of Jesus and when we shed this mortal body we too will be raised immortal.

By the age of twelve and maybe earlier, Jesus realized that he was not the same as other boys his age. He was aware that his Father was God and not Joseph, when he said, "Don't you know that I must be about my Father's business"? The boy was not God. The baby Jesus was not God. "A spirit does not have flesh and bone"(Luke 24:39). But the tiniest bit of matter in every fiber of his being that made up this man contained the Holy Spirit of the Son of God. This has been confusing because some have said, "Jesus is fully God and fully man, 100% God and 100% man". And while that may be true in some sense (the name of the 100% man is Jesus and the name of the 100% God is Jesus), it is confusing. When we say that the Spirit dwelt in the man, we have a tendency to think of a full sized spirit that looks like an apparition or "ghost" fitting into a man's body. For illustrations and diagrams it is drawn this way. Some even think that the Spirit didn't enter the body until the baptism of Jesus by John. It is more complicated to explain to children that God was in both cells at cell division but at some point as adults we need to understand that the matter, the flesh, of the body is not God and what caused the death of that body was the removal of the spirit from every intertwined part of his being. The body, the matter, the flesh, without the spirit is dead. He died. The Spirit didn't die. God didn't die. The body that was put in the tomb was not God. The physical, flesh and bone died when the blood emptied out of his body. And that blood after it left the body no longer contained the Spirit. It was just spilled blood. The blood doesn't do anything. But when it is outside of its body, it does signify that the body is dead and the death of Jesus did do something. It made him ready to be raised from the dead which paid for our sin and gave us a new life. When we say the blood of Jesus cleanses us from all sin, we mean his death and resurrection. When we say the preaching of the cross, we mean his death and resurrection. The flesh profits nothing. The blood without the Spirit profits nothing. The cross profits nothing. But in the Spirit, the death by the cross and the spilling of the blood and being resurrected profits everything, eternally.

There is something to be said about the voice. Jesus said, "My sheep hear my voice". When Jesus was speaking of the spirit in John 3, he said, "......you hear his voice". When Jesus addressed the Samaritan woman, at the well, he said, "I am the one speaking to you". The voice is spirit. Jesus said, "The words I speak to you are spirit.......and they are life" (John 6:63). Jesus is spirit, born of spirit, the eternal spiritual Son of God, the voice of God. Christ is the Messiah, a body, a man, but not of earth, from heaven, but born of a woman, a surrogate mother, with no DNA from Joseph nor Mary. But who knew? No one. Well, Mary knew and Joseph knew and at least by the age of twelve Jesus knew, but no one else knew that Christ Jesus the man, the son of man, was not the biological descendant of Joseph, but was the surrogate child of Mary. They all thought he was the "son of Joseph". This is why he referred to himself as the "son of man", because his purpose was resurrection not a virgin birth. He never announced to anyone that he was born of a virgin, or that Joseph wasn't his father. He only said to Mary about doing the Father's business. The virgin birth doesn't save anyone. It doesn't do anything. Without the resurrection we are lost. But, knowing of his birth from heaven helps us understand who he is.

His followers, his enemies, those who looked for fault, all, lovers and haters alike, all, thought that he was the son of Joseph, the carpenter's son. Not until Matthew and Luke were written and dispersed, probably fifty years after Jesus ascended did anyone find out about the virgin birth. It was not a requirement to become a Christian. It was not a requirement to be born from above and receive the spirit. It was not in the creed of the first church. I believe it. I believe that the body of the Christ, Jesus the Christ is divine, that he, that is his body, is made in heaven, but it is not a requirement to be a believer in the Messiah, then or now.

Some in ignorance have said that I disrespect Jesus because I don't believe that his flesh is God. I respect Jesus because he is God, Spirit, and he said, "the flesh profits nothing". I respect Jesus Christ because he is the Spirit of God living in a divinely created body. He is the Savior, the only mediator between God and man, the man Christ Jesus. He is God "manifested" IN the flesh. I would say that it would be disrespectful to say that God is flesh. God is infinite, eternal, immortal; flesh isn't. The flesh of Christ died. God can't die; he's eternal, he's infinite. God is not a man that he should lie nor the son of man that he should repent. God raised up Christ from the dead. The Spirit, the Son, that was in Christ returned to his Father and raised his body from the grave, resurrected. Because of this resurrection, we can live forever, we can be forgiven, paid for, accepted and have eternal life, because we can be born of spirit. Mary of Bethany believed Jesus and anointed him for burial and didn't go to the grave because she knew he wouldn't be there. That's why Jesus said that what she did should be spoken about in all the world every time the gospel is preached.

2

THE NAME

What's in a name? In this twenty first century we toss around names randomly because they sound good or are unique or we make names up for the same reasons. Sometimes we're named after someone like fathers and grandfathers as in "junior" and the "the third". But names in the first century were descriptive of the person's character. This is why Jesus and the apostles changed the names or added names to a person. Simon became Peter (Cephas in Aramaic, Petros in Greek but Peter in English), Levi became Matthew, Nathaniel became Bartholomew, Joses became Barnabas and many more. In the beginning before "woman" was named "woman" by Adam, before God took the woman out of the man (Gen 2:23), God called their name "Adam"(Gen 5:1-2); what an interesting passage. "In the day that God created man (adam in Hebrew), he made him in the likeness of God". God who? In the likeness of spirit? Or in the likeness of the body God had created for himself. I think the latter. He created them (okay so now it's "them") male and female, and blessed them and called their name Adam in the day they were created. So in the day (singular) that God created man (singular), he created him (singular) male and female (plural) and called their (plural) name Adam. Later on, God took the female side (translated "rib" but in Hebrew it means "side") out of man (adam) and made a female body. The male body that was left, named her "Woman". "and the man, the male body (adam) called the name of his wife (okay, so now they're married), the female body, "Eve" ("eM", in Hebrew) because she became the mother of all living (Gen 3:20). Later when "Eve" conceived and bore a son, she named him "Cain" (Qayin in Hebrew; sometimes meaning "acquired") because "I have gotten a man......" The point is, names mean something; at least that's the way it started. When Cain killed Abel (meaning "morning mist" which doesn't last long) Eve named her third male child "Seth" (meaning "restitution"). Noah means comfort. Abram means father and Abra-im or Abraham means father of many.

This would make an interesting study about names. The point here, though is to illustrate that names meant something. When God was asked his name by Moses (which means "drawn out", he was drawn out of the water), he said, "I AM" or "I am that I am" meaning, "my character, who I am, is my name, this is my name forever" (Ex 3:14-15). So, any of the names of God that we have been given all reflect something of his character. Later, in Exodus 34:6, Jehovah passed by before his (Moses) face and called out "Jehovah, Jehovah, God (el)........" Here we have what is called the "tetragrammaton" which only means "the four letters". These four letters YHWH or Yahweh or Jehovah

(JHVH) are used as God's name throughout the Bible. It may be related to I AM or Haya in the Hebrew dictionary and is thought to be some form of the verb "to be". Again it is a name that means character. However, the important part is next. After "I AM" says, "Jehovah, Jehovah, God", he says, "Merciful and gracious, slow to anger and great in goodness and truth, keeping mercy for thousands, forgiving iniquity and transgression and sin and not leaving entirely unpunished, visiting the iniquity of fathers on sons, and on sons of sons, to the third and to the fourth generation". That's a long name! God is describing his character and saying, "This is my character; this is my name". There are many compound names of "Jehovah" meaning different aspects of his personality such as "Jehovah Shalom", the Lord our Peace. But there is one name above all names because it means salvation to all of mankind and that name is "Jehovah-sua" or "Yahweh-shua" or Yeshua or Joshua or in Greek, Iesous or in English Jesus. There is something about that name but it's not the pronunciation of the English "Jesus", even if you drag it out, like "geeee zussssss". It's not the sound of his name, it's what it means in any language, Savior! "God is Savior", is his name and his character and his Son came in his Father's name. A look into the Lord's prayer in John 17 will show us that. The "Our Father" really isn't the Lord's prayer; it's the disciples prayer that Jesus taught them when they asked to be taught how to pray. And remember, they were in the old covenant; it's an old covenant prayer. The new covenant didn't start until Jesus rose from the dead. When Jesus prays, His prayer, the Lord's prayer, what we get is John 17. Jesus says, " I revealed YOUR name to the men whom you gave to me out of the world.......

they kept YOUR word. The words which you gave to me, I have given to them". No wonder the words of Jesus are Spirit, they are Father's words. "I came out from you. Holy Father, keep them in YOUR name. I kept them in YOUR name. I have given them YOUR word. YOUR word is truth. (Jesus said, I am the truth). I made YOUR name known to them. Jesus is God IN the flesh and his name is God's name and his words are God's words. When we say, "Jesus", we are saying God our Savior. Some have thought to honor God by calling their kids God's name. I think it's confusing and has made the sound "geezuss" or "hay sooss" or Joshua very common and in turn has caused us to not realize what the name means. Nothing wrong with naming a child that, but we confuse the sanctity of it with the common place of it.

In Judaism there is a term, "HaShem" meaning, "The Name". This is a reference to God because Jews think that saying God's name at times could be blasphemous, so they avoid saying it at all. In writings they will leave out letters so as not to be writing God's name such as "G-d" or "L-rd". The name is important to Jews. It is synonymous with God himself, because his name is who he is, his character. It was said of Jesus to Joseph, "You will call his name Jesus (Yeshua) for he will save his people from their sins"(Mt 1:21). Yeshua means Yahweh Saves or rescues. So Jesus' name does give us some idea of who he is. He is God. That is, the Spirit is God. As we discussed earlier, the Spirit was infused and intertwined into every minute particle that was Christ the man; but the particle, whether atom, or proton or the tiniest part was not God. As soon as the Spirit of Jesus left the man Christ, the man asked why have you forsaken me, because the Spirit of God had left him causing him to die spiritually like Adam. Then he died physically. Spirit never becomes flesh any more than fat can become muscle. I muse because years ago there were posters and magazines all over the gym about how to "turn fat into muscle". Okay, so now we know that can't happen and the new helpers at the gym are quick to tell us so. So we burn fat, and at the same time build muscle. Fat doesn't become muscle. It's not just semantics. In the Spirit world, it's not just semantics either. Spirit never becomes flesh. "But it says the word became flesh"(John 1:14). Actually, the text says the word was birthed in flesh and was in a tabernacle with us. The confusion comes from the number that Strong's assigns to the Greek word. The word is "egeneto", meaning to be birthed, number 1079. But the number that appears above that word is 1096 "ginomai" which does mean became. Why is this so important? Because we must realize that God is not a man, never can be a man, not even the man, Christ Jesus. God is a Spirit, the Holy Spirit and they that worship him must worship him in spirit and truth. To have any relationship with Jesus other than a spiritual one is knowing him after the flesh, which is idolatry. We relate to his Spirit not his flesh. "Oh, but I am in love with him and he is my husband". That will get you in trouble, especially you men.

Who is Jesus? He is Spirit. He is God. He is the generation of God, Spirit, the eternal Son of God. He is not a man. But the name of the Christ, the Messiah, the man was also Jesus. Jesus (God) is not the son of man. He was IN the son of man. He came in a body that he made for himself, but he is not his body, anymore than you are your body. Your body will die or put off mortality and when it does you will keep living. You will never die! Just change location. You will be in a different body and that body won't be you either. You are a spirit and so is Jesus. I am not saying that Jesus wasn't IN the flesh, that he was an apparition or only a spirit. He is Spirit in a body. "Everyone that confesses that Jesus Christ has come IN the flesh is from God" (1 Jn 4:2-3). He is in his immortal body now and will return as such. When he was here on Earth with his disciples he was in a mortal body and that body died. Jesus didn't die, any more than you will. His "temple" died and he raised it up in three days. At this point I can see how someone could take these words, edit them and make it say something I didn't say and that will probably happen. They did it with Jesus' words; why would they not do it to his followers also? They accused him of saying that he could destroy "the temple" and raise it up in three days. It's not hard to understand Jesus, if we think like him. But the only way we can think like him is if we eat and digest and meditate on his words, Father's words, Spirit and Life! It's always spiritual. Always. Oh Glenn, you spiritualize everything away. Actually, what I do is point out that Jesus "naturalizes" things that are spiritual to hide the meaning for those who will not think spiritually. We call them parables.

Jesus said, "And whatever you may ask in my name, this I will do, that the Father may be glorified in the Son. If you ask anything in my name, I will do it (Jn 14:13). "What did he mean? Because I've asked for a lot of things for me and others like health and life and like good stuff and added, "in Jesus name" at the end of my prayer request and .... nothing......silence. What's that all about"? Jesus said, (Lk 11:9ff) "Ask, and it will be given to you. Seek, and you will find; knock and it will be opened to you. For everyone asking receives, and the one seeking finds; and to the one knocking, it will be opened. And what father of you, if the son asks for bread, will he give him a stone, and if a fish will he give him a snake instead of a fish? And if he should ask an egg, will he give him a scorpion? Then if you being evil know to give good gifts to your children, how much more the Father out of Heaven will give.........(what?)....... the Holy Spirit to those asking him". "Oh. You mean ask for spiritual things. Like healing"? No, that's physical, natural, super-natural but still natural, carnal, super-carnal, flesh. "Like tongues"? No, that's physical, audible, hearing with your physical ears and spoken with your physical tongue. "Well, what then"? We ask for the Holy Spirit of Jesus to illuminate our thinking, to give us revelation of his word. "That's it? That's all we get"? He promised us "Eternal" life, life in the Spirit, was there more that you wanted? "Well, yeah, like no more suffering and pain and persecution". That's not Christ. "Well, how about prosperity and comfort and luxury like the King's kids"? I think you know the answer to that. When we ask in his name, we ask in his character. We ask for unity. We ask for understanding and wisdom from above. If any physical blessing follows, it's just God's kindness. We should never mistake God's kindness for what we deserve. He doesn't give us physical things to show his approval. He gives us his life, eternal life, to show his approval. "What about rewards in heaven"? Did you think they were physical, carnal, earthy? "The Muslims get seventy virgins, what do we get"? See where that thinking gets you? We get "rewards" in heaven. We get them openly, now, Abundant Life, now. It's in the Spirit. Let's look at the words of Jesus. In Matthew 6:4, (Please read the whole chapter, even the whole sermon) Jesus says, "Your Father seeing in secret himself will repay or reward you in the open (not later)". This isn't a statement about timing; it's a statement about secret and open. When you do your deeds in secret Father will reward you openly, now, in the spirit. In verse 6 again, "when you pray ....in secret,.......Father will reward you in the open". This isn't about "when", this is about "how". You will be aware that Father is rewarding you openly, now, in Spirit and others may or may not be aware. As far as eternal life is concerned, we all get the same reward, just like the parable in Matthew chapter 20. We have eternal life! And we get a new mind and a new body when we put off mortality. What else did you want? "Well, I just want to have more crowns than the others to throw at Jesus' feet". What? You're comparing your achievements to others. You don't want to look bad at "crown time". I don't know who started that line of thinking but it's absurd to think that the eternal Spirit would have anything to do with that. We need to start thinking spiritually or we'll never understand any of this............in the name of Jesus! But, what about the judgment seat of Christ where we get stuff. Well, that would be a chapter in itself. Suffice it to say that Paul said we would all stand before the judgment seat of Christ. I think that's true. But I already have. He also says that at the NAME of Jesus every knee will bow and every tongue confess that Jesus Christ is Lord, in that same sentence. I've already done that too and so have you (Rom 14:11, Phi'p 2:10-11, Isa 45:23). The point is "Don't judge". There is no more judgment for born from above believers in Jesus Christ (John 5:24)! I've already been judged, tried, found guilty, convicted, sentenced and deserved death. But my punishment has been paid! I'm free to go. So are you. It is finished! If we can believe that, we can begin to think spiritually. No more judgment. Like I said, it needs its own chapter, maybe in another book. Try *A View Worth Teaching* by this same author under the pen name of Tim Tyler.

I've heard "in the name of Jesus" added on to so many prayers by so many people until it begins to sound like a ritual, a mantra. And it gets faster as people in "corporate prayer" learn to pray really, really fast. They call it "rapid fire" prayer, " ....inJesusnameamen". Pray in secret. Pray in his character. Be still and know that He is God. Do not pray vain repetitions. "In Jesus name" is not the formula for closing a prayer. We're not supposed to say "in Jesus name" and then ask for things that are not his character. We're supposed to ask for things that are his character. "Father, Give us boldness to speak about the resurrection of your Christ"! That's a prayer "in Jesus name". "But it doesn't say, "in Jesus name". Exactly.

3

JUDGE NOT!

Jesus said it best, "Judge not, lest you be judged" (Mt 7:1). And remember, Jesus spoke to those that were still in the old covenant. Jesus taught them how to keep the law with new covenant principles. Later they would have to learn how to be led by the Spirit and walk in the new covenant with those same principles. So it has become necessary to include a chapter on judgment. John 3:17 says, "For God did not send his Son into the world that he might judge the world, but that the world might be saved through him. The one believing into him is not judged". Jesus said, "The one who hears my word and believes the one who has sent me has everlasting life and DOES NOT come into judgment"(Jn 5:24). There is, therefore, now no condemnation for those who are in Christ Jesus. There is no more judgment. But the argument shifts to a totally unrelated subject and continues with the wrong premise, namely, "Oh, but the judgment seat of Christ is to get rewards". Really?

Let's look at Paul's words, in context. In chapter 14 of his letter to the church in Rome he says, "Receive the one who is weak in the faith, NOT to judgments of your own thoughts.......do not judge the one eating.......Who are you judging another's servant?.........Why do you judge your brother? For all will stand before the judgment seat of Christ (at some point in our lives).........every knee will bow and every tongue confess to God (at some point in our lives). Each one of us will give account concerning himself to God (at some point in our lives). (And the conclusion?) Then let us no longer judge one another.....". Of course, read the whole chapter. The point is "stop judging". This has nothing to do with getting stuff when you die, not even crowns to throw at Jesus' feet. That verse, by the way, one verse, out of context sandwiched into this false concept refers to the twenty four elders. Are you saying that you are one of those (Rev 4:10)?

When we come to Christ as sinners, we come already being judged, by our past. He pays for our judgment and we bow ourselves to him and confess that he is the Christ. We came to the judgment seat of Christ. "But it says, We WILL come". It also says we WILL bow and confess and we've already done that. The point Paul is making is we all come to the judgment, not of each other but of Christ at some point in our lives and once that is done there is no more judgment (Rom 8:1). You are forgiven, cleansed, righteous, redeemed, holy, that's what saved means. Your spirit is alive to God and dead to sin. You are born spiritually of God. You are a spirit and you own a mind and a body. It's the spirit's job to convert the soul (mind), the renewing of the mind by meditating on Jesus' words, and that will transform our actions of the body. But the trial about our sin nature is over. We were found guilty, deserving the death penalty. Jesus took our place, paid our punishment that we WERE judged for at his judgment seat and made us new, new creatures in Christ, in the spirit. We didn't get a new mind or a new body. But who we are, the spirit being, is new. All things in the spirit are new. NO MORE JUDGMENT! Or Jesus death, burial and resurrection count for nothing if you think there is more judgment (2 Cor 5:10-21). However, there are consequences in the flesh, in the body, and we will receive the rewards and results of good and bad decisions in our bodies. We are forgiven, we are justified in the Spirit and there is no more judgment in the Spirit. But if we've done things detrimental to our health physically, we will reap. Or if we've followed God's food laws and God's instruction for living we will have rewards in the flesh, the body. Paul explains this in one of his more complicated messages on our earthly "house" and our heavenly "house". It requires multiple readings and meditation and I'm not sure I still understand all of what he was trying to say. But he does make a difference of things done in the body and spiritual judgment, i.e. "all things are new". Read carefully about his referral to the "judgment seat of Christ" in this chapter.

And then there's the other part of the mismatched sandwich. We get rewards in heaven (that's spiritual). You've already been given the greatest reward ever. And he earned it for you, a reward you didn't deserve. You already have eternal life. What else did you want? This false doctrine of getting stuff when you die has been falsely concocted out of Paul's letter to the church at Corinth. In the third chapter of his first letter he says, "I can't speak to you spiritually, you're

25

fleshly babes in Christ". That should be a clue. Divisions? Another clue. Then speaking about the denominations, i.e. of Paul, of Apollos, he explains that the rewards for planting and watering are believers that the Lord gave, that the Lord grew, so how can we take credit? The building is the house of God, you, the temple; the reward is lost souls coming to Christ. If they really come to Christ it is like gold, if not it is like straw. Jesus illustrated this in the parable of the sower. To think that God is going to give you more jewelry than your brother because you "won" more souls or preached better, that is the wisdom of the world. And then to call this the judgment seat of Christ is beyond stupid; Paul calls it foolish. Read the rest of the chapter about that. And then for the courageous read chapter 4. What does the spiritual life look like? Not prosperity, not esteemed among men, not without being wrongly accused. Let no one glory in men. But it is a small thing to be judged of men.

"But, (there's always a but) Jesus said," ....the son of man will give reward to each according to his works"(Mt 16:27). The works show the belief. "This is the work of God, that you believe into him whom that One sent"(Jn 6:29). The fruit shows the seed. Faith has works. And faith without works is dead (James 2:20). So according to works is according to belief and according to belief is spiritual not carnal. Can we grow out of baby thinking? "Glenn, that's just rude and arrogant"! Paul said it in his letter to the church at Corinth (1 Cor 3) and the author of Hebrews said it in the fifth chapter (Heb 5:11-14). We have this tendency to revert back to carnal baby thinking. We, I said we; I admit I could slip back into thinking in the flesh. It takes effort and meditation on what Jesus said to grow in the

Spirit and understand in the Spirit. We must continue in HIS word, then we will know the truth (Jesus) and the truth will free us (Jn 8:32).

"What about Matthew 25"? Here we go again. I used to listen to Keith Green music a lot. I still do but not as much. When you listen to music over and over, you get the song memorized without trying. That happened with some of his songs in my head. One was "The Sheep and The Goats" and another was "Asleep in the Light", it's counterpart. I still recommend listening to it, not for the music but the words. Then there's "The Prodigal Son Suite". I love his word choices and storyline but you can't get theology from songs, or the songwriter/singer. Song writers have "poetic license" and add and subtract things to make it rhyme or "fit". So the line Keith finishes with in "The Sheep and The Goats" is, "The only difference between the sheep and the goats is what they did and did not do". And it does seem that way. However, again, it's faith with works. Works only show the faith that motivates them. You can't earn the kingdom of heaven by working for it. However, if you have faith and compassion, that will move you to do the things in Matthew 25 that Jesus recognized. It's such an unconscious act that the ones "performing" the works didn't even remember doing it. And notice the "reward", "Come, ... inherit the kingdom prepared for you.....", no crowns, gold, silver, jewelry, mansions over the hilltop etc, nothing physical. The reward is Eternal Life in the Kingdom of Heaven. (Please read *They Heard What They Thought He Meant* by this same author). I realize that we have very little experience thinking spiritually but at some point we need to "work" at it. Reading and listening to Jesus speak is going to cause us to think spiritually. Nothing else will. All the carnal preaching with carnal examples and jokes and wisdom of the world will just keep it cloudy. Preaching should cause us to go to the "word", the words of Jesus, and meditate and ask "Lord, what does this mean"? And then listen and meditate.

Who is Jesus? He is God. He is Spirit. He is his word. He is the one speaking. He is not flesh. He is not carnal. He is the Spirit that is leading if we are willing to follow. The Spirit is willing but the flesh is weak. Jesus Christ has come IN the flesh. He has not come as flesh but IN the flesh. Jesus, the name of the man, the Christ, Messiah, that bore the spirit, is flesh, flesh from heaven, not of the earth, earthy. He is the Lord from heaven. Jesus is also the name of the body that Father created for himself. Father's name is Jesus and he gave his Son the same name. Jesus came in his Father's name. So when we say "Who is Jesus", we have to be clear about to whom we are referring. God made himself a body to show us an image of himself. Everything about Jesus, the man, is an image of God. The Christ illustrates how God suffers, cares, loves, pities and loves mercy and justice. We make the mistake, however, of sometimes thinking that he's like us and we would be more fair, caring, loving and execute justice better than he seems to be doing. Look at all the injustice in the world! "Where's God, Jesus, whatever you want to call him when children are being abused? Where's God when the helpless are suffering at the hands of perpetrators? Where's the justice and the care and the "voice of the voiceless"? We make the mistake of thinking that he means he will sort everything out on Earth and that he'll use us to do it. We were never called to change the world. We're not world changers. He thinks spiritually, and his rewards are spiritual. Life on planet Earth will be full of pain and suffering; that's just the consequence of mankind's bad choices since Adam and Eve. However, if we can begin to think in the Spirit we can also "for the joy that is set before us, endure……" (Heb 12:2).

4

LORD OR SAVIOR?

Of course, He is Lord and Savior. But, I've heard many times, "You know Jesus as Savior but do you know him as Lord"? That phrasing seems to say, "It's good that you know him as your savior, the one who died for you, took your place, and paid the penalty for your sin but are you obedient"? Somehow the horse always seems to find his way to the back of the cart and start pushing that cart instead of just walking and letting the cart follow. Some have argued that the horse is pushing the yoke and the yoke is "pulling" the cart. Really? It's a simple illustration not meant to teach the dynamics of the laws of physics, just an illustration. You can't really call it "sunrise" or "sunset" either, because the earth rotates on its axis causing day and night. We don't say, "Isn't that a beautiful rotation of the earth causing the daylight to turn colors and turn into night". The whole idea is about whether we make our lives better or he does. In the old covenant it was up to us to obey and God would bless us (pushing the cart). If we didn't obey, we would be cursed.

Sounds harsh. If the new covenant was that way also, what would be the "good news". What would be new? You can't put new covenants into old ones. The new covenant is new. It's not a continuation of the old. Jesus said, "Take my yoke upon you……my yoke is easy, my burden is light". Jesus fulfilled the old covenant. Fulfilled, in Greek it's "pleroo", Strong's 4137 which means to make full, to complete, to accomplish. Recently, I was told that "pleroo" only means than it's an example to follow. I don't know where that idea came from but it's just not in there. Peter says that we should follow Jesus' steps in his first letter (2:22) but he's speaking about suffering. When we suffer we shouldn't threaten. However, when it comes to the sacrifice for sin, there is only one, "…..who himself bore in his body our sins onto the tree; that dying to sins, we might live to righteousness; of whom, by his wound you were healed" (:24). Jesus paid, finished, fulfilled, accomplished the old covenant requirements for us and it is finished, done, paid in full. In the new covenant we are blessed and we obey because we appreciate his sacrifice and want to show our appreciation for him being our Savior. We were straying sheep, but now we are turned to the Shepherd and Guardian of our souls.

It's all about redemption. From the beginning God has always had a plan of redemption. We see redemption in creation and then re-creation in Genesis 1:1-3 (read *A View Worth Teaching* by this same author under the pen name, Tim Tyler, for details). Redemption (restoration, salvation) was in God's plan before he created Adam. Adam's sin was no surprise to God. He "covered" Adam and Eve with the skins of the sacrificed animals of that first blood sacrifice. He "saved" the human race through Noah. Again

God was not surprised; this was not an ad-lib response by God to the world gone mad. It was foreseen and God planned accordingly. Salvation of man was always planned. God is Savior (Yahweh Shua or YeShua) (Isa 45:21). His character is Salvation because he is Lord. He is never Lord without redemption (salvation, Savior). So, for those who thought he was only "Lord", he said, you don't know me and consequently, "I never knew you"(Mt 7:21-23), no relationship. The man who hid the talent "knew" him as "austere", "Lord", "a hard man", didn't know him as Savior, and his talent was taken from him and given to another (Mt 25:24ff). Many "know" him as Lord, God, Almighty, King, and so he is, but only Savior saves. Jesus (Ye Shua) came in his Father's name (character). Job knew him as Redeemer (Job 19:25). Paul writing to Titus says in chapter 3:4-6, "……the kindness and love of God our Savior toward man appeared,….. through Jesus Christ our Savior".

There is no name above the name "Jesus" (Yeshua). To know YHWH, JHVH, JeHoVaH, is to relate to him as our Savior. He is Lord. He is King. He is the Almighty, Creator of all the universes but more importantly he made a way for my freedom. He made himself a body and sacrificed it for my wrong doing and bought my freedom and yours. We love because he loves.

So in reality the question should be, "I know that you know Jesus as Lord, but do you know him as Savior"? You may know him as the giver of the ten commandments or the six hundred and thirteen commandments but do you know him as the one who keeps the commandments for you. You may know him as the law giver, the executive, and judge, but that also describes the government of the

United States. "The Government will rest on his shoulders and of the increase of his Government and peace there shall be no end….". But he is everlasting Father and Prince of Peace, the Wonderful Counselor, our Mighty God (Isa (9:6-7). His Government is founded on redemption. We will never qualify for his Kingdom on our own. The zeal of the Lord of Hosts will perform this because he is Savior, the name above all names, Jesus, Yeshua. And yet, some still insist on earning God's favor, by fasting, by praying for long periods of time, serving, being a missionary, (nothing wrong with any of that unless we're doing it to gain God's favor). "We will build…..we will change them…..in the pride of their heart," (verses (9-13); this is not "seeking" the Lord of Hosts. But God is Savior and "for all this his anger is not turned away……BUT HIS HAND IS STRETCHED OUT STILL"(verse 21). "The leaders of this people cause them to err" (verse 16).

Jesus said, "Take my yoke". The anointing (Messiah in Hebrew and Christ in Greek both mean literally to rub anointing oil) will remove the burden and break the yoke of the "Assyrian", the rod of my anger (Isa 10:5,27). "For my yoke is easy and my burden is light (Mt 11:30). "I will give you rest. You will find rest for your souls". Can you use some rest ….. something easy and light? No more anger of the Lord; no more judgment; no more wrath. God in Christ is the anointed one who brings rest. He is Lord and more importantly he is SAVIOR.

5

THE PRESENT

God describes himself as "I AM". When God appeared (as fire) in the burning bush to Moses, he said, "I am the God of your father". Not, "I was". "I am the God of Abraham, the God of Isaac, and the God of Jacob" (Ex 3:6). When Moses asked his name, "Who shall I say sent me"? God said, "I am that I am (Ex 3:13-14). Tell them, I AM sent you". As we discussed earlier God was saying, my name is my character, however we want to focus on a different aspect now. God proclaimed himself as "I Am" not as "I was" nor "I will be". He instructs us to remember what he's done and who he was to different people and he tells us what he will do and who he will be to us but his nature is always present tense, "I AM".

Similarly, Jesus said, "I AM". In many different ways he describes who he is, always using present tense. Especially in the gospel according to John, he IS. In the fourth chapter, he IS the one speaking to the woman; he IS the Messiah (4:25). In chapter six he says, "I am the Bread of Life.....I came down from heaven (6:35-38). I am the Light of the world (8:12). I am from above (:23). When you have lifted up the son of man, then you will know that I AM he (savior). I am the good shepherd (10:11). I and my Father ARE one (:30). I AM the resurrection and the life (11:25). I am the way, the truth, the life (14:6). I AM in the Father and the Father in me (:11). Father will send the Spirit of Truth; I will come to you (:16-18). I am the true vine (15:1). The point is to know who Jesus is we must focus on the present. It seems that we get off track when we focus on who he was, i.e. Judaism, or we obsess over the future, i.e. pre-milliniest, a-milliniest, or post-milliniest. "Are you pre-trib"? There are so many ministries that are pre-occupied with the "end times". I was part of one. Even now, the focus in the denomination I attend is on the "Blessed Hope", the second coming. The whole "Left Behind" fantasy is built on this pre-occupation with the future and has left us behind in our spirituality. Instead of being comforting, for many it has caused anxiety. There are "prophesies" and "the prophetic" and dates and times and seasons and whole seminars focused on Revelation and Daniel and Matthew 24. "When?" has become the most important question about Jesus. "When is he coming? When do I get out of here? "When will these things happen"? No one knows the future. No one. Only God knows the future and God in Christ, Jesus, is not focused on when; he is focused on "who" he is. He never answers "Why?" (asking "why" always leads to an argument, and there's no need for God to argue). He's not confined to time nor space so "when" is not the priority. His priority is "who". He asked his disciples, "WHO do you say that I

AM"? They asked "When is the end"? He said, "Don't be deceived"! It's not about "when".

Jesus is. Jesus is Father. Jesus is Spirit. Jesus is the Way, the Truth, the Life. Jesus is the Resurrection. Jesus is the Comforter. He comforts us with his presence and his peace. He doesn't want us to be anxious, to worry about tomorrow, i.e. "When is the great tribulation, the mark of the Beast, the rapture? When? When?"??? It's not about the future; it's about who. Who he is will see us through the past and the future. Jesus is Love.

Many of the so called "Messianic" ministries tend to focus on the past and the future, even to the degree of saying that the past predicts the future. So there are all these analogies floating around about Israel and America in prophecy. Some of the problem is the "tunnel vision" of how everything is determined by what happens in America (and of course America is limited to the United States to those prognosticators). All of the hate about homosexuality (which Jesus never spoke about), abortion, transgender rest rooms, and racism all seem to be focused on "American" problems. We want to see the future so badly that we look for fulfillments of "prophecy" to satisfy our curiosity, much like Peter saying that the day of Pentecost was fulfilling the prophecy of Joel. There was no fire and smoke and blood moon, and Joel said nothing about "tongues" which seems to be the most significant sensation for most "Pentecostals". Peter thought that this was about Joel's prophecy but it probably wasn't (read *They Heard What They Thought He Meant*, by this same author). Then there's all the teaching about the "Torah" and the Prophets. They say that we're supposed to keep all the feasts and rules and sacrifices, obey or else! Or else what? Is God going to revoke our salvation? Is our eternal life going to become temporary? Jesus IS our Passover (1 Cor 5:7). So we keep the feast with the new covenant not the leaven of the old covenant. And by the way leaven isn't bad. Leaven isn't sin. Jesus said that the kingdom of heaven is like leaven (Mt 13:33). They were told to use unleavened bread to remind them that when they were delivered from Egypt, they didn't have time to wait for leaven to make the bread rise. It's a reminder of deliverance. Jesus fulfilled the feast. He is our Passover; he is our Unleavened Bread of Life; he is the Firstfruits, raising from the dead. He "Tabernacled" with us. Certainly, he is our Atonement. He, Jesus, the Father, the Spirit is Shavuot (Pentecost). And the feast of Trumpets? In Revelation 1:10 Jesus says, "I AM the Alpha and the Omega, the first and the last......" in a great voice as a Trumpet. I think Jesus the Christ is the trumpet of God (1 Thess 4:16).

"Keeping" the feasts will give us insight as to all that Jesus fulfilled but rest assured it has been fulfilled, completed, all has been paid in full, finished. Keeping the food laws will help us be healthy but won't make you any more saved or holy. We should want to do these things because we are thankful not out of fear or condemnation. And I think God knew what he was doing when he prescribed one day of rest a week. It might be unhealthy to not rest one day a week but God's wrath won't throw lightning bolts at you if you don't. These works-driven, legalistic, judgmental dictators are like the little man behind the curtain in the "Wizard of Oz" bellowing out "I AM GOD!" to strike fear in the hearts of all that will listen. Love casts out fear. The new covenant is based on love and if we love him, it just follows that we will want to keep his commandments. Some have been called blameless and righteous, but "all" have sinned. No one has ever been able to keep the law. That's why we need a Savior. He keeps the law. Our Savior is not part of "all have sinned". He is not a descendant of Adam. He is from above. His body, soul and spirit are from above. "The second man is the Lord from heaven"(1 Cor 15:47). He knew no sin.

The old covenant is fulfilled. The new covenant is in force. Christ Jesus is the only mediator between God and man. We are forgiven. We are redeemed (Please read, *The Epic of Eden* by Sandra Richter). We are children of God. We are already in eternal life. Should we continue to sin that grace may abound? What? Of course not! Why would someone ask that? It would be like a man saving another man's life and then he who was saved wanting to see how much he could steal from his rescuer. Truly the rescued doesn't realize that he's been rescued and then in fact because of that may not be rescued at all. "He who has been forgiven much loves much". If you don't love much, well, maybe something didn't gel. The good news is we can start over. It reminds me of "Les Miserables". Father in Christ is always pursuing us. But our salvation doesn't depend on us "keeping" the law. It depends on our Savior keeping the law for us. It's not about the past; it's not about the future. It's about who we are in Christ.

The "Christian" community would be united if we focused on "who" Jesus is, not on who he was or who he will be. Presence is everything. He is present. When God said, "I AM the God of Abraham, Isaac and Jacob, they were already physically dead. He didn't say, "I was the God of Abraham", nor did he say, "I will be the God of Israel".

Our relationship is based on who he is now. God never changes, but we do. Our relationship is based on who he is now because of who we are now. He was the Lord. Now he is Lord and Savior to us. Some still know him only as Lord and that's not enough. We will never be accepted "into heaven" on our own merits, even if we kept the whole law and were blameless. All have sinned. All need a Savior. To know him as Lord is not enough, some will say, "Lord, we did mighty works in your name; and he will say, "I never knew you". That was "never'. "…..you workers of iniquity". Our salvation experience is relational, based on who Jesus is. It's not about rules and regulations, laws nor covenants. It's the new covenant. It's the new command, "Love one another, as I have loved you, love one another". How did he love us? How does he continue to love us? He gives. He gives expecting nothing in return. However, if we don't give, it's fruit that shows we haven't received. If we freely receive, we will freely give. We love because he loved us first. Commandments and precise rules and regulations are not necessary for the one who has been forgiven much and loves much. The law is for the law breaker. When we are born of Spirit, the law is written on our hearts. Our "want to's" change. Six hundred thirteen laws and their interpretations are for people who are looking for loopholes and ways to not love. If you love God and love your neighbor you will be keeping the law. All the past covenants were good but the new covenant is better. The new covenant is now, present. God is present. God in Christ Jesus is present. The "I AM" is always present (YHWH SAMMA, 3074 Strong's). Some spend too much time reminiscing about the "good ole days". Some spend too much time thinking about how great life will be "when I just get this or that", degree or spouse or bank account. Truth is these are the good ole days. It's cliché but it applies, "Today is a gift; that's why it's called the present". Jesus said, "I AM always with you". We can learn to walk in that comfort through any of life's hard circumstances, but we have to know him, his presence.

In John 14, Jesus tells us Father will send "another" Comforter, the Spirit of Truth. Maybe he meant an "other" form, because he says, "….he dwells <u>with</u> you and will be <u>in</u> you. I will not leave you FATHER-less! I will come to you". So, the Spirit of Truth, the Comforter (Parakletos 3875), the Holy Spirit is <u>with</u> you (in me) but will be <u>in</u> you (when I go). I, Jesus, will not leave you without a Father; I will come to you. The Spirit of Jesus is the Comforter, is the Father. I AM the Comforter which is the Holy Spirit whom the Father will send in my name. "I am in the Father and the Father is in me". And the Spirit will lead us by bringing to mind the things JESUS said. "The one seeing me has seen the Father"(:9). God is a Spirit. His name is Jesus. Jesus is (not was).

6

PRAYER

Like other words, when we say "prayer" we all mean different things. When we say, "pray" we mostly mean, "talk". And then there are all the different kinds of talking. Some would say prayer is asking. Some would say it's reminding God of his promises. That one's a bit confusing. Some say it's declaring things that already exist in the spirit world and haven't manifested in the physical world yet (like physical healing, "Oh, I've been healed; it's just not become physical yet"). We in Christian circles, begin and end our "prayers" with similar phrases, mostly, "Father God,……..in Jesus' name, Amen". But in more recent times, "praying for" someone has come to mean, "I'm thinking about you, hoping the best, wishing for better, and in more tragic circumstances it is coupled with, "I'm Sorry for your loss, we're praying for you". So it's meant to be sympathetic and comforting and for public figures it's sometimes abused to mean, "I hope everyone thinks I care", especially in an election year.

Okay, so why are we talking about prayer? Because our prayer life reveals WHO we think Jesus is. He's not Santa. He's not a politician. He's not sympathetic. He's empathetic and compassionate. He gives us his Spirit and Life and it's never couched in politically correct language. The way that Jesus gives us his Spirit and Life is by his words. "My words are Spirit and Life (Jn 6:63). Prayer is communicating with God. It doesn't matter if someone is listening to us and rating the prayer for its language or cool analogies or how fast we can rapidly fire words. We're supposed to pray in secret. That means intimacy between us and God. God doesn't even need us to talk. He knows what we ask before we ask it. We need to verbalize and express so that <u>we</u> know what we're asking for. The most productive way that we can communicate with God is by listening. When we listen, he is feeding our spirit, by his Spirit. We are born of the incorruptible seed, the Word of God and so when we hear the Word of God, Jesus' words, it feeds who we really are, spirit, born of Spirit, born of the Word. "But I don't hear God"! This seems to be the beginning of someone thinking that prayer doesn't work. We're expecting an audible voice or a sign from God. In the Old Testament, God related to man externally, with an external voice and external signs and miracles. When God revealed his nature in a body, in Christ, he was <u>with</u> them and continued to use externals. But when Jesus rose from the dead everything changed. It all went "<u>in</u>" ternal, "The Spirit of Truth will be "<u>in</u>" you. This is why we can't use Old Covenant scriptures to explain New Covenant concepts. The prophets desired to "see" the things we are capable of experiencing when we allow ourselves to think spiritually and not conform to the world's idea of prayer. The Holy Spirit, the Spirit of God, Jesus was with them on the outside, but when Christ was raised, the Spirit went inside; now he is in us working on the inside. This is why it was necessary for Jesus to "go" (Jn 16:7). Unless you are born of the Spirit, you can't understand this. If you don't understand this then get alone and ask God for revelation and wisdom and to hear his voice. That's a prayer he answers all the time. God always answers my prayers with, "Yes". We used to say God answers all prayers, but the answers are "Yes" or "No" or "Wait". But we've come to realize that there is prayer and then there's just wishing and hoping. If we ask for revelation and wisdom and growth in the Spirit that leads to peace, he always answers, "Yes". That is a prayer in Jesus name. I only ask for his Spirit and understanding and when I read or listen to the words of Jesus (red words), the answer is always there. This is how he speaks to us. These are his words. This is the Word of God. This is the Truth that makes us free (Jn 8: 31-32, if you continue in MY word). "Yeah, but don't you want healing"? I do, now more than ever; bodies don't last forever, but that's physical, flesh. The flesh profits nothing. We can't ask for flesh and tag on "inJesusname" and expect God to give us flesh. The sooner we learn that, the sooner we will begin to understand that he gives all that we ask for "in Jesus' name" (character, spirit). His answers are "Yes and Amen".

"Are you saying we all pray wrongly"? You can pray to Buddha or Vishnu or Krishna or Allah or the unknown god if you want to and I won't say it's wrong. You can pray for health and wealth and favor and for God to change other people and circumstances if you want to and I won't say it's wrong. Talking to God helps us. Talking to God changes us, our attitude and makes us feel better. However, if you want to "avail much", then we will have to pray the "effectual, fervent prayer of a righteous man". "As the Holy Spirit says, Today, if you will <u>hear</u> his voice and harden not your hearts......(Heb 3:7-8). The most effectual fervent prayer is listening to his voice, reading or hearing his words (red ones, the words of Christ). His Spirit will be speaking to our spirit, and something will be accomplished in the spirit whether we realize it in the natural or not.

"So, Glenn, don't you pray for other people"? I can't pray for other people. They must pray. I am not the mediator. I am not their high priest. I can agree with their prayers. I can wish the best for them. But if I'm not listening to God's voice, Jesus Christ, and they are not listening to his voice then it's just vain babbling and it doesn't matter how loud it is, or how emotional it is or how good the worship (really it's just music) is, or how fast it is; if we're expecting God to listen to us instead of us listening to him, then we're hardening our hearts because when he doesn't deliver the way we expect, we will think he's not answering our prayers, so what's the point? If we say, "In Jesus' name" at the end of our demands and we don't get the flesh we asked for, we think prayer doesn't "work". "You ask and do not receive, because you ask wrongly, in order that you may spend it on your lusts" (Jas 4:3, 5:16). In order for prayer to be effectual and avail much it must be based on his words and his character and then he always delivers. He is the Deliverer. "Pray for one another that YOU might be healed". Prayer changes the one praying; it's never guaranteed that the other person or circumstances will change. I find it interesting in James 5:16 that the example he uses is rain. It seems that

Elijah who is just like us prayed and the circumstances changed. Remember, Elijah was in the old covenant, externals. However, in 1 Kings 19:11ff, when YaHWeH passed by, Elijah experienced a tornado, an earthquake and a fire, but God was not in any of that. It was when he heard a still, small voice that he heard God and Elijah's attitude changed. Sometimes we become the instrument that God uses after we pray to be used to change circumstances and others may change as a result of seeing us change. I've heard that women shouldn't try to change their husbands. That if they ask God, he will change them, "Just turn them over to God, he can do more with them than you can". It doesn't work. God doesn't force change on anyone, no matter who's chanting incantations over them! God doesn't force his way into anyone's life. He's not a tyrant. Who is Jesus? He's a gentleman. He doesn't go where he's not been invited. He's not Santa, bowing to our Xmas lists (yes, please leave Christ out of Xmas, he was never part of that. Read *A View Worth Teaching* by this same author under the pen name of Tim Tyler). He is G-O-D, not D-O-G, obeying our orders and "reminders". He is the Word, the Word of God. He is his words, the red ones, the words of Christ, the words of life. He gives us all we need pertaining to life, eternal life, and godliness (2 Pet 1:3). He never feeds our flesh. Never. To ask for fleshly desires is futile, ineffectual, and avails nothing. We need to hear. Faith comes by hearing and hearing by the word of God.

"Who do I pray to? Father? Jesus? Father in Jesus name? Holy Spirit? God? God and Jesus"? I've heard these questions and not just from children. We pray to God. His name is Jesus. He is our Father. He is Spirit. We have been trying to differentiate between man and Spirit to understand who Jesus is. Jesus is the Spirit's name and also the name of the man. Because God lived among us in a body he made for himself and because that body died for our punishment, we are able to become his children, children of the Spirit. Through the death and resurrection of the body he made, the man, Christ, we have a mediator. We have an advocate. We have someone who is qualified to intercede on behalf of mankind to Father. The Spirit in Christ makes intercession for us.

This is where it gets touchy. Some think that we can intercede on other's behalf. We are not the mediator; there is only one. "Praying" for one another has become a buzz word and has no meaning. "Praying for you" really means wishing for you or hoping the best for you and is well intentioned and actually changes the heart of the person that is wishing and hoping. But wishing and hoping will never change circumstances or another person. Did we think we could change God's mind or influence his plan. God already knows everything that is going to happen. Before we had a mediator, God used the intercession of the prophets whom he spoke through. That was in times past (Heb 1:1-2). Jesus is our only mediator, that's who he is. God speaks only through his Son, now in these last days.

When Father speaks, it's like thunder. The voice is just there, in the air, everywhere, because Father is everywhere. He is Spirit. To be born of that Spirit, we would be everywhere also, but we're not. So, we use the term son or daughter to mean God's Spirit birthed in a body. It is still the same Spirit, but confined to a body. It is not all of the Spirit because Father cannot be contained. He is the Creator of the universe. The Holy Spirit of God in us is not the fullness of the Godhead. The Spirit in us bears witness that we are the children of God. The Spirit in us is a promise of greater things to come. The Spirit in us is a deposit, a guarantee. If we could use an earthly example which could never give the full spiritual meaning, it would be, God is like the ocean and we have one drop of that ocean water in us; a deposit. It is pure ocean water and fully ocean water but we're not full of ocean water. When God made a body for himself, he filled it full of ocean water. This is his <u>only</u> begotten Son. When Father which is Spirit which is everywhere speaks to the Son, the Spirit in a body, there aren't two or three spirits nor two or three persons in one God. The Spirit is one. This why Jesus, the Spirit, could only do what Father does. This is why the Son's words are Father's words (Jn 17:8). This is why the Holy Spirit is Father is Son. We are not "begotten" sons and daughters of God; we are sons and daughters of God according to promise. And we know that, when he shall appear, we shall be like him (1Jn3:2).

Some picture God, the Father as an older man talking to God the Son, a younger man and God the Spirit flying around like a bird (dove). Well, that might be art. That might be an artist's conception but just like we can't base theology on songs; we can't base it on paintings either. The Sistine Chapel is beautiful but it's not the Bible. When Jesus Christ was baptized in water by John, Father spoke; some thought it thundered. The Son, the Spirit in a body heard and understood. The Spirit (of Father) came down as a messenger (like a "dove"; at that time doves were used as messengers; we have called them "homing pigeons". Luke added, "in bodily form" to his gospel that he probably got from Mark's but he wasn't there and is quite possibly his own interpretation). Jesus the Christ is the ultimate messenger (Angel of the Lord) from God. If you've seen the Son then you've seen the Father. But no man has seen God at any time, because he is Spirit and you can't see a spirit. So again Jesus is not speaking physical. He never speaks physical; it's always spiritual. This is not just theology (man's attempt to study God) nor is it just a doctrine (one group's particular belief system). This is Spirit. These are Jesus' words and therefore Father's words, Spirit and Life. Father, Son, Spirit are three words that all refer to one God. There are not three spirits. There are not three persons. God is a Spirit. And if you want to worship him, it must be in Spirit and in Truth. Worship is how we live our lives; what we value; not how we perform on stage on Sunday morning. "We had good worship", what could that possibly mean? Can you have bad worship? Or was it just a bad performance? Worship is about "WHO". It's not all about that bass; it's all about Jesus. Do we depend on hearing his voice? (words of Jesus) Do we give? Do we love others as he loves us? That's worship. If we're not doing that then it's not bad worship; it's worshipping the wrong thing. "But I listen to Christian radio"! What? Wait, what? What in the world has that got to do with anything that we're talking about? I listen to all kinds of music on all kinds of stations and appreciate many forms of art, but that has zero to do with worshipping Jesus. Worship is what we do, not what we watch or listen to others do. "Well, I sing". Okay. Singing is not bad; it's just not worship, well, unless you worship your own singing. "Oh, but I worship God with my singing". Actually, what you experience is feeling good about singing to God. But worship isn't about feeling, it's about truth.

Who is Jesus? He is Spirit. Jesus is the Truth. Jesus, the Spirit, is in the man, the Christ whose name is also Jesus. "Don't you mean <u>was</u> in the man, Christ"? No! He's alive! He sits at the right hand of the Father. Hopefully, by now we know that Father doesn't have hands. Father is Spirit, Holy Spirit. Theologians call this anthropomorphism, the attributing of human traits to God. We've heard these terms: the eyes of the Lord, his hand is stretched out, the arm of the Lord, but it doesn't mean that God is human or physical. It's only man's attempt to visualize God (check out "carm.org" anthropomorphism: God relates to us in human terms, by Matt Slick). The resurrected body of Christ is alive, restored to its former immortal state. Where? I have no idea. It's in the "heavens" somewhere. But because he lives, all the saints that died before he rose, rose with him and live with him. And all the saints that die after he rose will live with him, or as Jesus put it, ".....will never die".

Prayer is communication in the spirit. God already knows what we are thinking and therefore anything we are about to say. The missing part of prayer is us hearing from him. "What about all the Old Testament examples of prayer"? They're old testament. "But". They're old covenant. We are in the new testament. "So we can't use them for examples"? No. "What about 1 Cor 10: 6? What do you do with that verse". I don't do anything with verses. Context, context, context. These are examples of what NOT to do! John 17 is a new covenant prayer. "What about the Our Father"? They were still in the old covenant. Check out Stern's commentary on the New Testament, Mt 6 about the "Lord's prayer". There was no new testament until Jesus the Christ was raised from the dead, and John 17 is all about that. Jesus taught his disciples how to pray in the old covenant, with new covenant promises and principles. He prepared them for what was coming. They had to figure out how to apply what they learned in the old covenant to the new (read "*They Heard What They Thought He Meant*" by this same author). "But, God sought for a man to stand in the gap and found none. So I'm going to be the one to stand in the gap for others". You can't. Christ is the only one qualified to stand in the gap; he is the ONLY mediator between God and man (1 Tim 2:5). Jesus said, "Search the scriptures (the law and the prophets and the writings, the TaNaKh) for in them you think you have eternal life, but it is they that speak of me"!

Every old testament promise points to the Messiah (Christ), the anointed one. Whenever God said, "Forever" as in keeping feasts and Sabbaths, they are kept forever in Christ. Like we said before, it's good to celebrate the feasts to remember and good to keep the Sabbath to rest and good to keep the food laws for health but it isn't sin if we don't. The New Testament is the fulfilling of the old testament and there is only one who could ever do that, Jesus Christ. Jesus is the Alpha and the Omega or in English, everything from A to Z. He is the beginning and the end. He is the author and finisher of our faith. He is the fulfilling of every covenant. He is all in all. I think Paul pretty much sums it up in his letter to the church at Collosse in chapters 1 and 2. We know enough not to require someone to be circumcised in the flesh, how is it that some modern day Judaizers want us to obey all the rules and regulations and sacrifices? The handwriting that <u>was</u> against us, the punishments for not obeying, have been nailed to his cross and died with him. He, not our punishment, was raised from the dead. He took our punishment and we are free. "Let no one judge you unworthy!" (Col 2:18). "…..Your life has been hidden with Christ in God,….." (3:3). If there is anything left from the old covenant that we are still responsible for keeping, then Christ did not fulfill the law (Mt 5:17). Jesus is our Melchizedek, forever. For the law perfected nothing. Jesus has become surety of a better covenant…….once and for all. (Heb 7:17-28, paraphrase, please read all of chapter 7).

Jesus is our Savior. What he has done, he has done forever. When we come to Christ and receive his sacrifice for our sins and transgressions and iniquities, we are rescued, saved from punishment. We become clean, washed, purged, brand new in the spirit. There is no more condemnation, no more guilt, no more shame, no more judgment. He will never leave us. We will never die. We will never thirst. We will never hunger. He doesn't come and go. This is new covenant. This is salvation. This is grace. Birth is eternal. Being born of the Spirit is eternal. We have eternal life. We live because he died and rose again. The "sinner's prayer" is for sinners. "Aren't we all sinners"? No. All <u>have sinned</u> (past tense), and come short of the glory of God, but now we are saints. Sinners are slaves to sin and cannot stop sinning. Saints are born of God and who they are, spirit beings, cannot sin (1 Jn 3:9, 5:18). The mind and the body sometimes sin but they are not slaves to sin to obey the lusts and affections of the flesh. Our Savior, our advocate stands as our mediator between us and the Holiest of Holies and protects who we are in spirit and renews our minds and one day will redeem our bodies.

But he never leaves us. The sinner's prayer is for sinners. We should agree with Jesus and realize that we ARE forgiven. We have been excused. I saw a sign outside a "church" that read, "Christ doesn't excuse sin, he forgives it". According to the dictionary, there's no difference. They are synonyms. To forgive is to excuse. But the concept in many churches is that we are forgiven, but.......... And that's a problem. There are no buts. "Well, but Jesus wants you to remember your sins and repent and strive and fast and pray and feel guilty for causing his death. Otherwise why would Keith Green have written the song, "Create in me a clean heart"? That song is the sinner's prayer right out of Psalms, when David sinned. That's not a saved person's prayer. He has already blotted out my transgressions, washed me completely from iniquity, cleansed me from my sin. My transgressions and sin is not always before me. He doesn't hide his face from me. He has already created a clean heart in me and he will not take his Holy Spirit from me. He will not cast me from his presence. He has delivered me from the guilt of shedding blood. I have a broken spirit, a broken and contrite heart, he birthed that (Ps 51). When my wife was a young girl, she would go to the altar every Sunday and "get saved". It's what she thought the church wanted her to do. Another friend of mine kept hearing, "I never knew you, depart from me". Both now have confidence in what Christ has DONE and no longer ask for forgiveness and salvation and joy. They have it. Please read *Victory Over the Darkness* by Neil T Anderson. Eternal life is eternal and it is free. Receive it and let it rule you. Guilt, shame and condemnation are not part of the true Christian life. They are not motivators. Who is Jesus? He is our forgiver. He has forgiven all our sin, past, present, and future. Receive this gift; it is free; there are no strings attached; but know that if you do, your life will change. "But all this time I thought I had"! Time seems to be a problem for us. God is not restricted to time. It is as if he planted a seed in some and they have been in labor (hard, striving, bone crushing labor) for years. And like in the natural if they were to die physically they would be with the Lord because they are unborn babies, not babies in mind or talent or knowledge but just not born spiritually. Some of these unborns are choir directors, Sunday school teachers, pastors, missionaries and evangelists. Their message is always about getting right with God, which is good for the sinners within earshot, but personally they are conflicted and not at rest or peace with Father. When I came to Christ, he saved me. I did nothing worthy of earning his salvation. But it is a done deal. "How do you know"? Because that's who he is. Now, if my life hadn't changed, if there were no fruit, then I would be like one of the examples in the parable of the sower. But a changed life or even the beginning of a changed life shows fruit and fruit is the difference in the parable. "By their fruits you will know them". "So if I'm a Sunday school teacher and have been "saved" for twenty years but still feel guilty and feel like there's the possibility that he might say "Depart from me" to me and like I need to repent every day and strive in "prayer" and ask him to cleanse me every day, do you think that I'm not saved"? It doesn't matter what I think, that's between you and Jesus. What I do know is that while you are in the spiritual womb, so to speak, even though you've taught and done mighty works in his name, and may not be BORN you are still an unborn child and God doesn't do abortion. So you are saved because you're a child but you're not enjoying the joy of salvation. Or maybe you are born and have heard so many "wrong" messages, that it's just a feeling that you are somehow guilty. If we focus on Jesus' words our thinking will change and consequently our feelings will change. By the way if you think you would be embarrassed if anybody knew this, then don't share it. "What"? Yes. Don't share it. Salvation is between you and Jesus only. And all that work you've done is not in vain. Somehow we think time matters to God. "I've been saved since blah, blah, blah". It's not a race. It's not a contest. Nobody wins. But everybody wins. Who is Jesus? He's your Savior. He's your deliverer. He's your best friend. He is God and he loves you because that's who he is. The only thing that pleases him is his children. He loves giving birth. Let him.

7

THE MAN

Jesus is God's name. God is Spirit, Holy Spirit. Jesus is also the Christ's name. The Messiah that was promised, the one Moses spoke of, the one David wrote about is a man, a messenger, a body. The Spirit, the Holy Spirit, the Father, the Father's Son dwelled or tabernacled in that body, the body of the man whose name was Jesus. As the angel told Joseph, "You will call his name Jesus, for he will save his people from their sins". Mind you it wasn't "save his people <u>in</u> their sins", but "<u>from</u> their sins". God in Christ came to abolish, destroy sin in the flesh. And he did. Jesus, the eternal Son, came in his Father's name and subjected himself to a flesh, blood and bone body. He gave up immortality, omnipotence, omnipresence and omniscience to be confined to a body. As we spoke about before, this is not two spirits. This is the Spirit of God in a body, which is different than the omnipresent God because it is impossible to contain all of the Spirit of God in a body. This is difficult to explain and difficult to understand, but in our limited finite human understanding, all we can say is, as Paul puts it, "For let this mind be in you which also was in Christ Jesus, who subsisting in the form of God thought it not robbery to be equal with God, but EMPTIED himself, taking the <u>form</u> of a slave, having become in the <u>likeness</u> of men, and being found in fashion <u>as</u> a man, he humbled himself having become obedient until death, even the death of the cross"(Phi'p 2:5-8). It's difficult because we can't use words like "part" of God, or "a portion" of God, because God doesn't have parts. God is a Spirit. So God says, "My Son". The Son is the Spirit of God, confined to a body by God's own choosing, but has always existed, eternal.

The body, he made for himself, however, has not always existed. It is flesh and bone. It has a beginning. It is the created not the Creator. God is the Creator, the Spirit, in a body that he created. It is this man that we speak of when we say, "Christ". This Christ is known in the old covenant as "Melchizedek". We should read the letter to the "Hebrews" especially chapters 1 through 10, many times to get an understanding of "how great a man this was" (Heb 7:4). I will be quoting from it, but to really understand we should meditate on the whole context. I think a commentary on the "book" of Hebrews might be our next book; we could call it, "Behold the man"! But for now we'll skim across the epistle to get a "bird's eye view" of who the man, Christ Jesus is.

Hebrews 1:1, In the past God spoke through the prophets, but he doesn't do that anymore. Now, he only speaks to us IN his Son. He is the heir of all. He is the firstborn. He is the express image of his essence through whom all things were made. He became or was made mortal so that he could taste death for us. He "took hold of" the seed of Abraham. He was assumed into Abraham's lineage. All Christian religions would agree that Jesus was not the son of Joseph but neither did he come from Mary's egg. That would make him a descendant of Adam, which in turn would make him born with an inherited sinful nature like us. But he knew NO sin. This body started as a pure seed of DNA from the original body God made for himself in heaven before the world was created and was planted by the Spirit of God into Mary, his surrogate mother. He was tried by suffering. He wasn't tempted to sin. God said that the children of Israel "tempted" him in the wilderness. Now we know God can't be tempted. So it means something else; they tempted him on the outside, describing their action but God was not tempted on the inside, describing his action. Jesus was tempted by the tempter, describing Satan's action but he was not tempted on the inside, describing his own action. They heard God's voice and ignored it. They heard the gospel but didn't listen and thereby didn't believe. Today, you can hear the gospel preached and still not listen and not believe. Listening requires meditation, meditation on Jesus' words. Jesus is our high priest. He has been tried in all suffering but not tempted to sin. He came to destroy sin not be tempted by it. There are high priests from among men but to the Son, God said, "You are my son, today, I have begotten you". You are after the order of Melchizedek. He suffered. But, to the recipients of this letter the author said, "......you are dull in hearing (not listening, not meditating), infants (fleshly thinking), not skilled in the word of righteousness". "Are you saying if we don't get this we're infants and dull of hearing"? No. What we're saying is, that it requires reading and meditating many times to understand. I mentioned to someone once about a passage in the Bible. He said, "I've read the Bible". Once? That's it? Once? We think that's enough? No, I would say if we are not meditating on Jesus' words every day, we're starving. Give us this day our daily Bread of Life. Jesus entered the holy of holies and paved the way for us to enter because he is Melchizedek. He is the king of righteousness, the king of peace (salem, or shalom, Hebrew for peace), WITHOUT father, WITHOUT mother, WITHOUT genealogy, nor beginning of days on earth, nor having end of life. But he became mortal and was able to die and be resurrected for us. Jesus, our high priest, is not according to the order of Aaron; having been born of a woman of the tribe of Judah. The law changed. This is why so many "Messianics" struggle with "Hebrews". Hebrews 7:12 says, "….. the necessity of a change of law occurs". And in verse 18ff, " …..a voiding of the preceding command……..The law perfected nothing. Jesus has become surety of a better covenant", ……ever living to intercede for us. He didn't destroy the law, he fulfills it. The requirements have been met.

Jesus is our high priest. He is our true tabernacle. He is the pattern shown to Moses on the mountain. He is the mediator of a better covenant……a new covenant, God's laws written on our hearts and minds. And for those who are his people, those who are born of God and have the law written on their hearts and minds, who desire to obey, he will not "remember" their sins. In the saying "new" he has made the first "old" and it is near disappearing (Heb 8:13). "But Christ having appeared as a high priest of the coming good things, through the greater and more perfect tabernacle not made with hands, that is, <u>not</u> of this creation, nor through the blood of goats and of calves, but through his own blood, he entered once for all into the Holies having procured everlasting redemption (9:11ff). Because of this he is the mediator of a new covenant, ...for Christ did not enter into the Holies made by hand, types of the true things, but into Heaven itself.....and shall appear a second time.....". This is how great this man is. Because of this I feel like I owe him my new life. That's why the song says, "Jesus paid it all; all to him I owe......". Not because Jesus says we owe him, it is a free gift, but because the writer of the song feels this enormous gratitude and feels like he owes him. He came to take away sins. "For this reason, coming into the world, he says, "Sacrifice and offering you did not desire, but you prepared a body for me" (10:5). He is the mediator, the only mediator of the new covenant. He mediates for us; we can't mediate for ourselves or others. He is the only man who knew no sin and yet became sin for us. We can't do that. The greatest story ever told is about the greatest man that ever lived and lives again. He was flesh and bone and blood. When his blood was emptied out of his body, he died. God didn't die. The body died. When the body was raised incorruptible, he appeared to his disciples and said, "A spirit doesn't have flesh and bone as you see me have"(Lk 24:39). I suppose blood is not needed in a resurrected body. In a natural body, the life is in the blood, but in a spiritual body, the life is in the spirit. Jesus is the name of Father. Jesus is also the name of the body he created for himself. The blood of Christ (or the death of Christ proven by his exsanguination, death by loss of blood) and resurrection purifies us but only through the eternal Spirit. He is the mediator. He is the Christ. He is the man. The eternal Son,

Jesus, the Spirit, is in the body, the man, we call Jesus, the Christ. He is strong. He is the strong one. When we are weak and we depend on him as our mediator, our advocate, our redeemer and savior, then we are strong, strong in the Lord. When we realize that we are weak, he is strong in us. If we think that we are always strong, we have no need for him. "But I've always been a strong person able to bear the burdens of others and never let anyone see me show any weakness. That's why I never cry. I would never let anyone see me cry". Jesus wept at Lazarus' tomb and he cried at Gethsemane with strong crying and tears. But he is the only one who could overcome death. He alone is strong and the sooner we realize that we all are weak, we can be strong in the Lord. His grace is enough for us. "My strength is made perfect in weakness" (2 Cor 12:9). When I may be weak, then I am strong. Crying is cleansing and results in freedom. Don't be afraid to let them see you cry. You will be stronger. Don't be afraid to let them see you worry. "Um, Jesus said, "Don't worry". I know. But we do. He said, "Don't worry about clothing and food". But there are tons of other things to worry about. It just means were afraid. When we're afraid, we're weak. Courage is not the absence of fear but the action of moving forward in the presence of fear. Cast your burdens upon the Lord. Bring worry and anxiety to him. Don't hide it and pretend it doesn't exist. Share it and confess that we trust Jesus to be strong on our behalf. Life is not Facebook. You don't have to keep up appearances to be a good Christian. A good Christian knows he's weak and our Champion, our Savior is strong and he will never leave us. Expressing weakness is not confessing sin. Weakness is our own human frailty, not disobedience. "I'm not the best speaker", is weakness and he will help us speak with boldness. "I cut people to shreds with my tongue" is sin, not weakness and needs correction and repentance not strength. When we are weak, he is strong. When we sin, we are forgiven, but that should result in gratitude and obedience. In the old covenant we were required to obey to be forgiven; in the new, we are forgiven and it makes us want to obey. I am not "the man"; he is "the man". I am not the mediator; he is the mediator. I am not strong; he is strong. Consider how great a man this is.

Peter said, "Jesus the Nazarene, a <u>man</u> from God, having been approved among you by powerful deeds and wonders and miracles which God did through him in your midst…..."(Acts 2:22). Paul said, "For God is one, also there is one mediator of God and of men, the <u>man</u> Christ Jesus….."(1 Tim 2:5). And again, "Great is the mystery of godliness; God was manifested IN flesh" (1 Tim 3:16). And again, "God was IN Christ, reconciling the world unto himself" (2 Cor 5:19).

There have been many men called "Great". Some have conquered the known world. Some have been the greatest boxer or other sports figure. As I write this there is one who has promised to be our champion and solve all our problems if elected. Make no mistake; there is only one "Great one" and he's not a talk show host. He is Christ Jesus, the only <u>man</u> who could die for your punishment and mine and make us free. And that's the Truth! In Romans 5:12 and following, Paul explains, but even that needs explaining. He says, "….. sin entered the world through one man….. But the free gift will not be like the offense, for if by the offense of the one many died, much more the grace of God, and the gift in grace, which is of the one <u>man</u>, Jesus Christ, did abound to the many". Again Paul writes, "When the fullness of time came, God sent forth his Son, born of a woman……"(Gal 4:4). The Son of God is Spirit but often visited Earth in the immortal body he made for himself, Melchizedek, King of Righteousness. But when the fullness of time came, the body became mortal and was birthed through a surrogate mother, not the seed of Adam nor the egg of Eve, to be born without sin, so he could die for the sin of the world, all of mankind. As it is written, "For he made him who knew no sin to be sin for us, that we might become the righteousness of God in him"(2 Cor 5:21). That which is born of Spirit is spirit and that which is born of flesh is flesh. Jesus the Spirit, is born of the Spirit. Jesus the man is born of the flesh. All Pilate could see though was Jesus born of the flesh when he said, "Behold the man". He is not fully God and fully man. He is fully God IN fully man. The deity of Christ is that not only did the man Christ contain the fullness of the Godhead bodily but the body, the LIKENESS of sinful flesh was also made completely in heaven and did not have the death sentence of sin from Adam. But God is not a man and never will be. God will never be flesh. The body is from heaven but it's not God. One day we will receive a body from heaven (remember 2 Cor 5) but it won't be God either. It will be from God, but it will only be a "house". "So who do we pray to"? We communicate with Spirit. If Jesus is your "homeboy" or your "boss" is a Jewish carpenter, you've missed something. And "Co-Pilot"? Where do they get this stuff from? I am considering how great a man Christ is but worshipping the Spirit, Jesus. In John's first epistle, in the fifth chapter, verse seven, we have an interesting deviation from the text. Except for four or five of the most recent manuscripts, all the oldest manuscripts do not contain the words from: "in heaven ....to ....on earth". In other words in the oldest manuscripts it reads: "For there are three bearing witness, the spirit and the water and the blood; and the three are to the one", making the point that Jesus was a man, not an apparition, or as John says "Jesus Christ has come IN the flesh." Later the lines about the Father, the Word, and the Holy Spirit were added to justify a "trinity" doctrine. Check out the footnotes in the NIV Bible and the Nelson Complete Study System concerning the "NU" text and the "M" text. The oldest manuscripts are the most reliable. "We know that we are of God, and the whole world lies in wickedness. And we know that the Son of God has come, and has given to us an understanding that we might know the true ONE, and we are in the true ONE, in his Son Jesus Christ. This is the true God, and the life everlasting. Little children, guard yourselves from idols"! (even the idol of worshipping the flesh of Jesus).

8

LOVE

God is love. Jesus is love. Who is Jesus? He is Love. Simple, profound, elegant. However, we all have different ideas of what love is. There is parental love, romantic love, love of food, some people even love their work. So when we say that Jesus is love, what does that mean? Biblical references will probably get us close to understanding how it is that God (whose name is Jesus) is Love.

We can start with 1Cor 13, as would be expected. Often quoted in weddings and pictured on various plaques and paintings to decorate one's home 1Cor 13:4-8 seems to sum up in Biblical language what the definition of real love is. When the Bible says that God is Love, I believe it is this kind of love that it is speaking about. In another place, Paul writes about the fruit of the Spirit, the fruit (singular) of THE Spirit. In his letter to the church in Galatia he says, "The fruit of the Spirit is Love, and then he lists other characteristics of this fruit which is love (Gal 5:22). In 1 Corinthians he defines love in many ways and these ways coincide with the characteristics that he lists in Galatians. For example: Joy, love rejoices at truth; Peace, love is not easily provoked; Longsuffering, love suffers long (or patience); Kindness, love is kind; Goodness, love thinks no evil; Faith, love believes all things; Meekness, love does not pursue its own things; and Self-Control, love does not behave indecently. We seem to be on the same page, and the one thing that seems to sum up what the fruit of the Spirit yields is love. The Spirit is Love and Love never fails. Jesus never fails. When we say, "Jesus loves you", it's not romantic love. He's not your husband or your boyfriend. His love is not only sympathetic but empathetic. Although close in meaning "sympathy" or same feeling is more about me, how I feel and commiserating together; "empathy" is more about me understanding you, how you feel and encouraging you. His love is not the kind that is concerned about how he feels. Often people marry because the other person makes them feel good. Well, what happens when they don't make us feel good anymore? Feelings come and go and often without notice. The love of Jesus is not fleeting. It's not a feeling; it's an action. And greater love has no man than this, that a man would lay down his life for us. Many men and women have laid down their lives for others, but none except Jesus was a flawless, blameless life that could pay for all our wrongdoing. He gave up his immortal body to enter into the world to die for us. No one else has or could have done that. Remember he was immortal before he was born of a woman.

Jesus is Love. Jesus, the man is the physical representation of what love is. Jesus, the man, is the visible image of the invisible God. God is Spirit whose name is Jesus, is Love and the body he made for himself to "tabernacle" in or dwell in has demonstrated how Love behaves. Love gives life, eternal life, and life abundantly. Love is Spirit and it is life. Love gave mankind a second chance; no other beings of God's creation get that. Love forgives. Mankind is the only part of God's creation that is offered a Love relationship, not the cherubs, not the seraphs, not the twenty four elders, not the beasts before the throne, only man. I suppose that's what really set Lucifer off. When he found out God's plan for a creation in which God would have a love relationship, Lucifer rebelled and then fell; fell right into the plan for the redemption of mankind. God knew Lucifer would rebel. God knew man would sin. We can't understand infinity or omniscience but we believe that God is infinite and he knows everything. When he created Lucifer, he knew. When he created Adam, he knew what would happen. The first creature he created was a body for himself and he knew then that the man, Christ, the body, that he created for himself in which to dwell on earth would one day die for the punishment of mankind's sin. Not that God forced Lucifer to fall. Not that God caused Adam and Eve to sin. But God did cause them to choose. He placed the "tree" of knowledge of good and evil in the middle of the garden, and the "tree" of life in the middle of the garden for Adam to choose. The tree of knowledge wasn't a fruit tree, neither was the tree of life. We speak of people having fruit, good fruit or evil fruit. The tree of knowledge had bad fruit and Adam and Eve took part in that. They ignored the one bearing good fruit but later the "tree of life" rescued them. I wasn't there and I can't explain the details of what happened but these weren't apples and oranges. Was the "tree" of knowledge of good and evil Satan? And was the "tree" of life Jesus Christ? I think so, but can't prove it. Jesus told us that a good tree bears good fruit and an evil tree bears evil fruit. And he was talking about people (Mt 7:17-20).

Now we need to talk about something else, "semantics". It seems whenever we bring up stuff that is controversial or requires explaining someone says, "Oh, it's just semantics", like that would mean something. Semantics is the branch of linguistics and logic concerned with meaning. There are a number of branches and subbranches of semantics, including *formal semantics*, which studies the logical aspects of meaning, such as sense, reference, implication, and logical form, *lexical semantics*, which studies word meanings and word relations, and *conceptual semantics*, which studies the cognitive structure of meaning. All that to say that words have meanings. When I was younger raising teens, some of my kids used words wrongly because of not knowing the real meaning of the word. When I would correct the usage of the word they would say, "Well, that's how I use it". So, yes, it is good to know the correct meaning of a word, semantics, before using it, or we couldn't communicate. However, when a disagreement of concepts occurs, we can't just jump to "confusions" and say, "it's just semantics". There may be something wrong with the logic or lack of logic that's causing the disagreement not the meaning of the words. Some would argue anything just for the sake of arguing and when they get stuck use the get of argument card, "It's just semantics", and "We're saying the same thing just different words". Simple. The argument comes to a screeching halt and nothing was learned, which is the reason for the word "semantics" coming into the conversation in the first place.

Another tactic for not learning is, after arguing for several minutes to just say, "Well, I don't want to argue". If someone says, "The Bible says" when the Bible doesn't say and you point it out, you're liable to hear, "It's just semantics" and if you point out that there's not a difference in meaning, you'll probably hear, "Well, I don't want to argue". Well, we can argue a point without being argumentative. How else are we going to hear a different view than what we already have, in other words, learn? Here's a couple more "I don't want to learn" phrases, "Why do you always have to be right"? and "Can't you just listen to me and let it go"? What these phrases really mean is "I've already got my mind made up, don't confuse me with the facts". As I write this the Democratic and Republican conventions are being aired on TV, a perfect example of not wanting to learn anything on either side. It's concrete; all mixed up and permanently set. If we stop learning, we stop growing. Love causes growth. Growth is a sign that something is living. All of Jesus' parables have to do with birth and growth in the Spirit. If we aren't growing, we're dying. There's no coasting in Christianity. Jesus said, "My Father works and I work here too". There's always work, action, motion, growth, love in the kingdom of heaven. The Sea of Galilee is alive with motion, water from Mount Hermon flowing in and water in the Jordan River flowing out. The large lake is teeming with fish and wildlife. The Dead sea however, is dead. It is stagnant. There are large deposits of sediment, mostly salt, because although it receives, it doesn't give. Good clean, alive water from the Jordan flows into the Dead Sea and it just sits and stagnates and evaporates; it doesn't flow anywhere. Be a Galilee. Learn, flow, give, grow........love.

Real love, biblical love, godly love, agape love is life. There is romantic love and family love and self love which are all part of our psyche or mind and emotions and necessary. But we're talking about eternal life, life in the spirit and that life produces spiritual love. The whole reason we love is because God first loved us. He birthed in us the capacity to love. We have received the ultimate gift and when we realize that, we want to live so others can have that gift also. God used someone or many someones to give us that gift and now that we are born into eternal perfection and are sealed there is no more to achieve for ourselves. We're in. When we realize that, we want to help others connect and stay connected to Jesus. It would be like winning the 100 meter race and then going back and helping others win their races and events. We're not competing anymore. We won. And we didn't do it, he did. It is a free gift. But make no mistake; Jesus won't take your salvation from you. The devil can't steal it from you; neither can you "lose" it. You can't do anything to lose it as you didn't do anything to "earn" it. "You mean, once saved, always saved"? I mean once born always born, unless you reject your salvation. You are the only one who can reject your salvation. No one can take it from you but if you don't endure until the end you could end up like Esau, rejecting your birthright. "So how do we endure"? Learn, flow, give, grow …..LOVE! Love endures all things. Love never fails. Faith, hope and love remain, but the greatest of these is Love. Pursue Love!

Read the Bible. Fellowship with other believers. Give to the body of Christ and to the poor. Study. Pray. But more than all these, listen. Listen to the words of Jesus Christ, sometimes found in red. Prayer is communication and communication is getting each other's thoughts into each other's minds. God already knows our thoughts so the only way to improve our relationship with him is to get his thoughts in our minds. Let this mind be in you. The only way to think like God is to think like Jesus Christ. And the only way to think like Jesus Christ is to know him. And the only way to know him is to hear his words and remain in them; meditate in them. Once you begin to "hear" him speak to you through his words you'll be addicted. Nothing will be as important as hearing him. You won't be wondering, "Who is Jesus"? You'll be able to tell others who he is and what that means for them. You'll be able to keep the new commandment, "Love one another as I have loved you; Love one another"!